KINGDOM OF SPECULATION

Books by Barbara Goldberg:

Kingdom of Speculation
The Royal Baker's Daughter
Marvelous Pursuits
Cautionary Tales
Berta Broadfoot and Pepin the Short

KINGDOM OF SPECULATION

Poems by
Barbara Goldberg

Accents Publishing • Lexington, Kentucky • 2015

Copyright © 2015 by Barbara Goldberg
All rights reserved

Printed in the United States of America

Accents Publishing
Editor: Katerina Stoykova-Klemer
Cover: *Portrait 09*, digital artwork by Catrin Welz-Stein, *catrinwelzstein.blogspot.com*

ISBN: 978-1-936628-31-5
First Edition

Accents Publishing is an independent press for brilliant voices. For a catalog of current and upcoming titles, please visit us on the Web at

www.accents-publishing.com

CONTENTS

Foreword / ix
The Kingdom of Speculation / 1
The Blood of a King / 2
Interregnum / 3
Slough of the Seven Toads / 4
Three Caskets / 5
At the Foot of Mount Misery / 6
The Heart of a Princess / 7
The Highway of Bones / 8
The Barker's Call / 9
Two Mangled Heaps / 10
The Early Childhood of Grief / 11
The Master of Chance / 12
Two Solitudes / 14
Grief Gets a Dressing Down / 15
Grief in Tatters / 16
No Small Feat / 17
The Birth of Compassion / 18
Small Wonder / 19
Chance Is Off / 20
Luring the Tiger / 21
Bandits All / 22
The Nature of Nature / 23
A Great Darkness Falls / 24

Acknowledgments / 27

FOREWORD

Welcome to the Kingdom of Speculation, dear readers, where *to steal an egg is to be beaten to death,* where *the graves of thieves are stacked like dominoes at the edge of town.* Welcome to the world where *chickens are revered, the most popular tunes / being hymns composed in their honor.* All you have to do is to open this book on a poem such as "The Barker's Call" and you will be enchanted. You will meet a princess *looking no more / like a princess than you or I.* You will meet Rodrigo, the Master of Chance. You will walk the *highway of bones,* and you will understand—like any human should—that Grief is *a surly, birdlike boy / who refuses to cry.*

In this book you will be under the spell of imagination that is truly impressive. But, more than that: you will fall in love with Barbara Goldberg's syntax. The way her sentence works against her line-breaks, creating fireworks, is a fairy tale in and of itself. Her poems are magical, not because they contain princesses and ravens and thieves of eggs. They are magical because their music grabs us and won't let us be. Their music has mystery of *six ravens* which *descend, celestial consorts of the dead, six ravens / who peck all the eggs save one, the ivory / Egg of Perfection.* Indeed. The secret to true music cannot be understood. It can only be applauded.

ILYA KAMINSKY

for my small wonders,
Gabriella, Madeleine, Sandy and Vincent

THE KINGDOM OF SPECULATION

Eggs coddled or poached are the food
of choice in the Kingdom of Speculation

for eggs are exceedingly rare and stored
in brooders. Brooders are guarded by men

who sport checkered vests and twirl
batons. To steal an egg is to be beaten

to death and the graves of thieves
are stacked like dominoes at the edge

of town. The rich feast on eggs
while the poor eat dumplings which look

like eggs but sink in the belly. Chickens
are revered, the most popular tunes

being hymns composed in their honor.
In this Kingdom only the weather is fair

and the air holds the scent of cardamom.
Overhead birds fly ignored, singing

an ostinato: *what if, what if, what if.*

THE BLOOD OF A KING

Once there was a certain King who pricked
his thumb on the thorn of a white rose.
Even the blood of a King runs scarlet, and did.

It ran and ran. It ran until all the rivers
and streams in the kingdom ran red. Then
the fields turned red and everything that grew

in them, corn, barley, soon the milk from the cows
and goats. And when the Princess wept for her father
her tears ran red. And then he died. He was buried

without pomp in the red earth, leaving
the kingdom in disarray—the Queen
took to muscatel and her royal bed, attended

by seven simpering knaves. The Minister of Finance
retired to the counting house to count up the money.
There was plenty. He issued an edict forthwith

forbidding the pleasures of hunting, dancing, racing
and conversing, then galloped by horseback out
of the kingdom, followed by a pack of 42 mules

hauling coffers of sovereigns. And thus
the wealth of the kingdom was carted away.
The kingdom languished under a shroud

of thirst. But over time a particular flower
thrived, which the Princess, a botanist, named
amaranthus caudatus, love-lies-bleeding.

INTERREGNUM

Three years have passed. Three years
the vermilion kingdom has slumbered
underwater, lulled by a hard rain

that has fallen without intermission.
When the flood subsides, the land,
rinsed clean, approaches its original

state. Now the Princess embarks
on a journey with nothing more
than a mission: to collect and classify

each plant for the royal archives.
With love-lies-bleeding tucked in
her bosom, she heads for the cardinal

points to learn precisely what
has survived, what the land sustains.
The farther she travels, the more vivid

the palette—verdant fireweed, yellow
loosestrife. Her spirits lift when she spies
a new species, tubular, two-lipped,

pale pink, she names it *beard's tongue*.
Giddy with naming, the Princess is likewise
immersed in her own anonymity.

SLOUGH OF THE SEVEN TOADS

The elation of naming, that dispassionate
stance, of course it could not last. As all

first steps it was bound to lead to that first
misstep, that attenuated fall through ebony

branches into the Forest of Indifference. Oh
how to define the pain of it, the eclipse

of sky, the scales that seemed to sprout
over her eyes, the petals of love-lies-bleeding

wilting in that thicket of night? Then a headlong
plunge into the slough of the seven toads

and there defiled by false iridescence, the barter,
the intrigue, the back and forth, that rough

exchange, the petty puffery of fame,
the flat inspection of their malachite eyes.

THREE CASKETS

Along came three suitors. She found them
all lacking: casket of silver, casket of gold,
casket of lead. She considers lead—

he's heavy. If she ties herself to him
she'll sink. But oh the liquefaction
of the sheets, and oh wouldn't she expire

in the rapture of that deep. Silver
flashes slick off the tundra, elusive
as flight. In his wake, a killing

freeze, an excess of courtesy. At first
gold's glitter dazzles, his overflowing
pockets. Fortuna is his mother, but

his expression's a trifle stupid. How's
a princess to rule with no casket
for her jewels? At this hour the shops

are closed. The graveyard beckons
but the coffins are sealed with old
remains. She's been here before,

her legacy these ruby scars, those
smoky pearls. Let her string them
on a flaxen thread for all to see.

Let them incite the mercy of thieves.
Let her step forth in the ancestral land
accompanied by her own two hands.

AT THE FOOT OF MOUNT MISERY

A snaggletooth crone at the foot
of Mount Misery offers the Princess
a bargain: a pillow filled with the down
of the poke-leaved milkweed, softer by far

than feathers. And this guarantee: if
she but lay her head on it, she will suffer
no more disturbing dreams, not ever, no
spiders or lizards crawling on the knee,

no apparitions of the dying King. The price?
A mere pittance: that the Princess transport her
to the Harpy Haven rest home where the crone
can bask in luxury. By a simple transformation

she'll turn herself into an imbricated milkweed
seed and stuff herself inside the pillow.
She swears the Princess won't feel a thing,
why, she won't weigh more than a thistle.

THE HEART OF A PRINCESS

The Princess has the heart ... well,
the heart of a princess. Yet studying

the crone, her snaggletooth, her shifty
expression, she cannot help but feel

a pinch of reservation. If she takes her
on she might never reach her destination—

there is so much work to do, and all
her own subjects. On further reflection

the Princess has no wish to forfeit
her dreams, not even the most appalling.

As for the weight, she seriously doubts
the crone's powers of transformation.

She'd guess the crone weighs in at a full
seven stone, one for each day of the week.

With all the grace she can summon, and not
without sorrow, the Princess refuses.

THE HIGHWAY OF BONES

Under no stars on the highway
of bones, the Princess broods

on her losses: the King is dead,
the Queen is dead, her beloved

nursemaid Gertruda demented, she
who spun fanciful tales of dwarfs

with spurs on their boots. Farewell
Gertruda. Thus intent, the Princess

trips on a femur, falls, cracks open
her head. Demons appear to snatch

that part of her soul called *memoria*.
Out flies the King, the Queen, Gertruda,

and everything she ever knew, that one
and one makes two, that two from two

is naught. And there she might lie
till this very day had her shadow not

lassoed the demons with a skein
of dreams, thus releasing memoria

which recomposed in the Princess's skull,
who awoke, remembered, refreshed.

THE BARKER'S CALL

The moon had slipped down in the sky
when the Minister of Finance returned
to the Kingdom of Speculation. There

he dismounted, and following the barker's
call, wagered all on the contest between
Reason and Passion. Reason was splendid

in spangled tights, flexing his fabulous
biceps. The Minister promptly lost
his heart. Passion, that kleptomaniac,

stunned him with her ardent gaze, her
see-through froufrou. She stole
his breath away. Finding himself

with no heart or breath, the Minister
expired on the spot, not even his pack
of mules or their cargo could save him.

TWO MANGLED HEAPS

Noon in the kingdom. The sun
fixes its steady gaze on Reason

and Passion, two mangled heaps
on the floor. They gingerly rise,

bones aching from lying so
fiercely entwined, then wend

their way to a sequestered inn
where they hold a secret

rendezvous, where they kiss and
make up, tending to each other's

wounds, as they are wont to do.

THE EARLY CHILDHOOD OF GRIEF

And from the loins of Reason and Passion
springs Grief, a surly, birdlike boy

who refuses to cry. No gurgling, no babbling,
no scattershot foray into the dense

and dissonant world, choosing instead
to stay mute, to absorb it all

through his eyes, his parents, their singular
deadlock. Passion has no patience

for Grief, nor Reason, the stomach,
so consumed are they by each other.

Grief grows in time as time grows
in him, each nanosecond adding

to his girth. Soon he's wearing
a polka dot vest on his way to school

where he loses his marbles, is pelted
with dumplings. He finds refuge lying

flat on his back in an open field
where he studies the sky, the inhabitants

thereof, at ease in that recitative,
consoled by the heavenly undertones.

THE MASTER OF CHANCE

The Princess, looking no more
like a princess than you or I,
lifted one shabby foot over

the border and stepped into
the province of Chance. And there
was accosted by a hard-boiled

brooder. Oh he was chic, very chic
indeed, with gleaming spats, pomaded
mustache and a voice that was pure

basso profondo. *Dear Madam,* he purred,
*I am Rodrigo, the Master of Chance. Be
my bride. Polish my coffer, keep*

count of my chickens. The Princess,
as you must know by now, was no fool
and recognized a royal coffer

when she saw one. To be the wife
of a brooder held no appeal, but yes,
she wanted to see the coffer, and when

she did, knew it at once for the one
belonging to her father. The brooder,
watching her stroke the coffer, told

how a gambling man lost it to Passion,
*a woman in my employ, as is everyone
in this Kingdom, for I am the Master*

*of Chance, I cut the deck, declare
what's wild, as you are my dear, my Balkis,
my Hatshepsut, my true Queen of Hearts.*

TWO SOLITUDES

The coffer of course was filled
with eggs, for eggs were exceedingly

rare in the Kingdom. They could have been
scrambled for all she cared. To win back

the coffer was her task, and for that
she needed to hatch a scheme. Without further

ado the Princess left, making her way
to an open field where she met Grief and lay

down beside him. And of the speechlessness
that passed between them, there is this

to say: it was as though the choked-back
sorrow each contained was given

shape—that perfect orbit where
two solitudes embrace.

GRIEF GETS A DRESSING DOWN

And what did you expect, she asked,
to be loved unconditionally, coming
first, always first in their loyalty?

to be spoon-fed all the fruits, the fragrances
of an exotic vegetation? that trees bloom
perennially, and the sun always warming

never burning? that fungus be pliant,
always weathering your footfall?
And when this effulgence was not

forthcoming, you clamped your jaws
shut, a gesture louder than speech
that seethes atone, atone, for

I am not at one with thee.

GRIEF IN TATTERS

Tra la tra la her searing words
so startled Grief that he began
to sing *tra la tra la* to drown

her out, her incessant meddling.
Tra la his notes rang out so pure
they seemed to burst from Artesian

springs, so pure the starlings froze
midflight, flustered by virtuosity.
What crumbles into tatters is

Grief's dusty musty mourning cloak
much like a brittle chrysalis
tra la la la tra la la la

NO SMALL FEAT

No small feat for Grief to doff
his mourning cloak, the velvet
heft of it, and its scarlet naught

emblazoned in cross-stitches, insignia
for *not enough*. He might easily
have kept it on, remaining wrapped

in sorrow, for surely there is enough
sorrow in this world to dwell in. If we
could earn a crown for every soul

we found shrouded in despair, why
we'd be richer than a dozen kings!
Which explains why moths grow fat

and tailors are by nature cheerful,
day in, day out, their nimble fingers
stitching habits of our own choosing.

THE BIRTH OF COMPASSION

And in the very act of singing Grief
expires, dissolves into that grander
scheme called Melody. Now christen

him Compassion, a sturdy, upright boy
whose heart quivers to the pulse
of every living thing, once

it's free from the stranglehold
of private past. For all
when born are torn asunder

as on the second day, the waters
from the sky, where nowhere
is it claimed that it was good,

but on the third day, it is said
twice, as if to make amends, or as if
to honor pain and not diminish it,

to let it have its own day. And why
does the Princess feel her knees
grow weak? Perhaps because even

an ode to sorrow makes a joyful noise.

SMALL WONDER

The Master of Chance is the only master
in the Kingdom of Speculation, sole keeper
of odds, of track, of coffers. Three cheers

for the Master, his fine mustache! All Hail
Rodrigo's Formulation: *probability equals
N/(p-n)*. His subjects have it engraved

on their foreheads, bow down in awe. Yet
Rodrigo is barred from the carriage where travel
Deep Conviction, Absolute Certainty, and that

crusty crusader, Crux of the Matter, who merely
pass through this way on their way somewhere
else, and each in a first-class compartment.

It rankles. Snubbed as master non grata.
Even a blind boy who aims at a hawk can
sometimes by Chance manage a hit. Small

wonder he finds the Princess enchanting.
She brings the blood to his chilly cheeks,
a fact for which there is no accounting.

CHANCE IS OFF

One day Rodrigo receives a gold-embossed
invitation, signed in the florid hand

of Deep Conviction—his presence most
respectfully requested at a Congress

of Masters. The topic on the agenda
is one of mutual concern: namely,

the weather. Savage whirlwinds threaten,
courtesy of the Great Lord Chaos. Since

Chance is his great-grandnephew, his input
is deemed indispensable. Fortuitous Chance!

Unlike his great-granduncle, he has
seven holes in his body, can therefore

delight in the tasty prospect of a brief
sabbatical. He packs his most elegant duds

in a flash, wraps three cloisonné eggs
as a housewarming gift, and is off.

LURING THE TIGER

What Chance cannot guess is the Princess
herself has penned the parchment, using

an ancient stratagem: *lure the tiger down
from his mountain in order to capture*

the mountaintop. Substitute coffer. Convert it
to planter and lay to rest the dried petals of

love-lies-bleeding, the stubborn ghost
of her father. Though dead for some time

he still holds court in the four chambers
of her heart. Then to commence the radical

restoration of the royal archives. Thus
she justifies her craftiness. With duped

Rodrigo en route to Conviction's castle,
the Princess moves to reclaim her Highness.

BANDITS ALL

Reason, somewhat looped on peach julep,
is scanning the headlines on the veranda
when Compassion comes calling. *Father,*

he says, *I need your muscle.* Flattered,
Reason (what say now, his son can talk!)
rises to the occasion. He finds Passion

in the kitchen, looking for all the world
like a fishmonger's wife (faded flannels,
flip-floppy sandals), stewing her own

coq au vin. Reason asks her to give them
some rope. Then all set out for Chance's
manse, a regular nuclear family. Together

they commit breaking and entering, together
slip the rope round the coffer, together hoist
it out the back door. The Princess cleans

the lid of the coffer, spreads over it a red
checkered cloth. Passion prepares an elaborate
brunch: cold cherry soup studded with dumplings,

deviled eggs, of course the coq, frosty tumblers
filled with parfait. Ignoring the rain
they sit down to a sumptuous feast. And eat.

THE NATURE OF NATURE

After debating the nature of nature
over a pipe and a demitasse, after

helping the Princess sort through her
satchel, its slapdash array of botanical

specimens, Reason pries off the lid
of the coffer using two thumbs. Alas!

One whiff of the rotting eggs and they
collapse in a swoon. Six ravens descend,

celestial consorts of the dead, six ravens
who peck all the eggs save one, the ivory

Egg of Perfection, which cannot be cracked.

A GREAT DARKNESS FALLS

What the Princess can't guess is that Deep
Conviction in fact has convened such a Congress
where Chance pops in, an unexpected

guest. In time the Princess arrives
with the King's coffer, a fertile bed
for her cuttings and seeds. Inside

her purse, the Egg of Perfection, her ticket
home, price for safe passage. A mighty wind
whips through the castle, extinguishing

light. Confusion ensues—the Princess
falls into the arms of Deep Conviction
while Chance, that fickle cavalier, fumbles

for Absolute Certainty, wild for her
creamy complexion, her dainty neck.
Crux takes a shine to the tender

lad Compassion. All is poised for
an *ever after.* Sing praise to the Great
Lord Chaos, his enabling dark. Praise

to the touch of a choice companion.
And praise to the Egg of Perfection
glowing in the folds of a lady's purse.

ACKNOWLEDGMENTS

Beltway Poetry Quarterly, "The Kingdom of Speculation," Arlington Arts Center, first prize

Innisfree, "The Early Childhood of Grief"

Paris Review, "No Small Feat," "Slough of the Seven Toads"

The Royal Baker's Daughter (Felix Pollak Poetry Prize) "No Small Feat," "Slough of the Seven Toads," "Small Wonder," "The Early Childhood of Grief," "The Kingdom of Speculation," © 2008 by the Board of Regents of the University of Wisconsin System. Reprinted courtesy of the University of Wisconsin Press

I am grateful to the National Endowment for the Arts, Maryland State Arts Council, The MacDowell Colony and Virginia Center for the Creative Arts for providing me with the time and space to write many of these poems.

www.ingramcontent.com/pod-product-compliance
Lightning Source LLC
Chambersburg PA
CBHW021454080526
44588CB00009B/844